Yankee Stadium
In Your Pocket

A FAN'S GUIDE

SO-EIG-768

Kevin T. Dame

ISBN # 0-9640946-2-2

Published by Baseball Direct
Central Falls, RI

Design by Christine Dame Yoshida
Layout by Janice Garsh
Illustrations by Ryoji Yoshida, Kevin Dame, and
Christine Dame Yoshida.

Second Printing
Printed in the United States of America

This book may be ordered directly from the publisher by sending a
check or money order for $9.95 per book plus $2.00 shipping and
handling to:
Baseball Direct, P.O. Box 6463, Central Falls, RI 02863.

Contents

Chapter Three: Baseball Basics

Chapter Four: Life Beyond Yankee Stadium

Chapter Five: Fanhood Challenge

Preface

Any sports fan worth his salt is familiar with the expression "the house that Ruth built." It refers to Yankee Stadium, once upon a time the world's most spectacular sports complex. It now serves as a veritable baseball shrine, as decades of baseball history have unfolded within its walls.

This book is about Yankee Stadium, one of the few remaining ball parks from baseball's early years. In an era of fabricated nostalgia, Yankee Stadium serves as a reminiscent reminder of the way baseball used to be. A night at Yankee Stadium is probably little different than one fifty years ago when Joe DiMaggio was terrorizing opposing American League pitchers.

This book is not about boring history or "who cares" trivia. It is a user's guide to Yankee Stadium, written for you the Yankee Stadium parishioner, to help you get the most out of your experience at the game. Whether it's a helpful tip on where to park your car, or a review of the "Yankee Stadium Beer Rules," you'll be coached step by step through the entire experience.

We invite you to fill out the survey in the back of this book and send us your ideas and tips on how to enjoy the Yankee Stadium experience. Your unique perspective will help us to continually improve this guide and help fans enjoy their experience all the more.

As you join the more than two million fans who enter Yankee Stadium each season, use this guide to its fullest and you'll be guaranteed a great time.

CHAPTER ONE

PRE-GAME PREP

Yankee Stadium Oath

Before we begin, every Yankee Stadium visitor must learn the basic rule of fanhood – the Yankee Stadium oath:

> *On my honor, I promise to cheer on my Yankees, to devour hot dogs and peanuts, to properly execute the wave, and to soak in the fresh air, smells, sights, and sounds of Yankee Stadium, until I am truly at peace.*

Baseball psychics have determined that the ghosts of Ruth, Gehrig, and other Yankee greats are pleased when an entire stadium of Yankee fans recite this oath before games.

Yankee Stadium History

During the summer of 1920, New York Giants manager John McGraw watched in anger as the crosstown rival New York Yankees (who played their home games at the Giants' Polo grounds) began to outdraw his Giants. Led by Babe Ruth's .376 average and unheard of 54 home runs, the Yankees drew 1.3 million fans at the Polo Grounds as fans clamored to see the Yankees' new star. As a result, the Giants demanded that the Yankees hit the road and build their own stadium, and Yankees owner Jacob Ruppert jumped at the opportunity to build what would become baseball's most famous stadium. The team began the process of searching for a construction site for a new stadium, and ultimately settled on a spot in the western section of the Bronx. In less than a year, Yankee Stadium was built: a magnificent, triple-decked structure designed to showcase Ruth and other star players pillaged from the rival Boston Red Sox. Opening day occurred on April 18, 1923, and the Yankees defeated the Red Sox 4-1 behind (you guessed it) Babe Ruth's first home run of the season. Yankee Stadium soon became known as "The House That Ruth Built."

The original design consisted of three concrete decks extending from home plate out to the left and right-field corners, a single deck in left field, and wooden bleachers in center and right fields. In 1928, second and third decks were added to left field. Further upgrades occurred, as the wooden bleachers were replaced with concrete in 1937, and auxiliary scoreboards were added in the late 1940's.

In its early years, Yankee Stadium was a quirky place. The

team erected a green screen in centerfield, which provided Yankee hitters with a better hitting background. Of course, when the opposing hitters stepped to the plate the Yankees would often remove the screen, leaving the visiting slugger with a hitting background of white-shirted bleacher fans. Years later, deep left center field would feature three, in-play stone monuments which honored Yankee great's  Gehrig, Huggins, and Ruth. During one game, manager Casey Stengel watched as a well hit ball sailed past the Yankee centerfielder and rattled around among the monuments. As the beleaguered fielder struggled to corral the elusive ball, legend has it that Stengel yelled, "Ruth, Gehrig, Huggins, someone throw that darned ball in here, now!"

Yankee Stadium's most dramatic renovation occurred during a two year period from 1974-1975, during which the Yankees played their home games at nearby Shea Stadium. During this major undertaking the field dimensions were altered, the famous monuments were relocated to Monument Park behind the left field fence, and most of the stadium's beautiful copper, art deco frieze was removed from the roof facade. (Some of this frieze was preserved and today hangs above the bleachers in centerfield).

Yankee Stadium's largest crowd occurred in 1928, as 85,265 fans packed the place to watch the Yankees face the powerful Philadelphia Athletics. The smallest crowd ever to take in a game in the Bronx occurred in 1966, as 413 fans willed themselves to endure a game against the Chicago White Sox. Yankee Stadium's current capacity stands at 57,545.

Yankee Stadium Fast-Facts

Yankee Stadium
161st St. and River Avenue
Bronx, NY. 10451
Ticket Information: (718)293-6000
www.yankeees.com

Home games: 81 games (April to October)
Game times: 1:05 pm (day), 7:05 pm (night)
Radio Coverage: WABC 770 AM
TV coverage: WNYW channel 5 Fox and
MSG network

Selecting a Game

The art of selecting the perfect game is based upon five important factors. Whether it be for your family, the date you're trying to impress, or a business client, considering these five factors will help make your time at Yankee Stadium all the more enjoyable:

1. Weather and time of day
2. Time of season
3. The opponent
4. Pitching match-ups
5. Yankee promotions.

Weather

It's most important to be comfortable! The prospects of shivering in the face of cold, gusting winds, squinting through your rain-soaked glasses, or passing out due to 90-degree temperatures can all be eliminated if you dress properly for the weather and time of day.
In April, and again in September, you may need a winter jacket, a sweater, and possibly a hat, gloves, and even thermal underwear. Remember, you'll be sitting outside in one place for three hours. For those of you who think that drinking alcohol will keep you warm (college students, pay attention) — you're wrong! The alcohol slows down your metabolism and opens up the pores in your skin. You could actually get hypothermia!

In the middle of the season, during New York's warmest weather, shorts and T-shirts suffice during the day, while a wind-breaker is usually a good idea to have with you during night games. Certain areas of the stadium (especially the bleachers) are exposed to strong sunshine, so during the summer make sure to bring a supply of sunscreen. Loge and main reserved seats are mostly shielded from the rain, and during a rain delay you will be protected. However, if you are in an unprotected zone (bleachers), make sure you bring a small umbrella just in case of rain. (See "Picking the Best Place to Sit" on page 18 for more information.) Even when rain is forecasted — a common occurrence in New York summers — grab a wind breaker and umbrella and head to the stadium. It's still worth going because many games are still played after a short delay. You can get a better idea of the likelihood of a game being cancelled by calling the Yankees at (718) 293–6000, or by listening to WABC 770 AM on the radio for the latest weather information.

Time of Season

The time of season strongly influences ticket availability, the size of crowds, and the general atmosphere inside the stadium. The first month of the season is an exciting time for fans (especially opening day), but seats are a bit easier to get due to the colder weather. During the dog days of summer (late July through August), games are often sold out, yet many fans lose a little interest and turn their attention to barbecues, trips to the beach, and members of the opposite sex. In September, Yankee Stadium can be slower if the team is out of contention, but is buzzing with excitement and filled to the brim with rabid fans if the Yankees are battling for the divisional crown. Because of Yankee Stadium's allure and charm, its slowest moments are still characterized by healthy attendance.

Opponent

"Who are the Yankees playing tonight?"— a common question asked by fans considering a game. Games against arch-rivals (Red Sox, Mariners) are more exciting and sought after than games against other teams (Tigers, Devil Rays). In fact, attending a Yankees - Red Sox game at Yankee Stadium is one of the most intense experiences in sports.

Pitching Match-Ups

Predicting a game's starting pitcher can be done a few days before the game. This can be accomplished if you know the team pitching rotation. For example, if the Yankees' starting rotation is (1) Mussina, (2) Vazquez, (3) Brown, (4) Contreras, and (5) Lieber, and Mussina pitched on Monday night, then you can predict with reasonable certainty that Brown will pitch on Wednesday night, two games after Mussina. Star pitchers are always worth going out of your way to see if you appreciate good pitching. If you want to see lots of hits and runs, your best bet is to pick games with the worst pitchers. While the pitching match-ups add to the flavor of the game, most fans generally select a game without concern for the pitchers.

You can also read the Pitching Match-Ups in the Newspaper: In the newspaper sports page, look for a section entitled "Today's Probable Pitchers/Latest Line" (usually found below the standings). Quite a bit of information can be found in this section, including the game times. Most games begin at 7:05 p.m. on weeknights, and 1:05 p.m. during the day.

Beginning with the left column, you can identify the teams playing one another (the first is the home team). Next to each team is the name of the pitcher starting the game. In parentheses next to each pitcher is R or L, indicating right or left-hander. The time of the game is shown next, along with the odds for those confident enough to bet on a

		Time	Line	1998 W-L	1998 ERA	Team Rec.	1998 vs. opp. W-L	IP	ERA	Last 3 starts W-L	IP	ERA	AHWG
TODAY'S PROBABLE PITCHERS													
AMERICAN LEAGUE													
BOS	Martinez (R)	1:35	-220	8-2	3.31	10-5	0-0	0.0	0.00	2-1	17.2	6.62	14.8
At TB	Johnson (R)			2-3	5.67	6-4	0-0	0.0	0.00	0-1	11.1	8.74	15.1
KC	Pichardo (R)	1:05	-115	2-6	5.96	4-3	0-0	0.0	0.00	2-1	16.0	3.94	13.5
At DET	Hattiger (R)			0-1	6.75	0-1	0-0	0.0	0.00	0-1	5.1	6.75	15.2
TOR	Hentgen (R)	1:35	-115	7-4	4.35	8-7	0-0	0.0	0.00	0-0	20.1	3.54	13.7
At BAL	Ponson (R)			1-4	5.28	1-3	0-0	0.0	0.00	1-2	18.1	2.95	11.3
MIN	Morgan (R)	2:05	-115	3-2	3.95	6-8	0-0	0.0	0.00	1-1	16.0	3.38	12.4
At CHI	Bere (R)			3-6	5.94	5-9	0-0	0.0	0.00	1-1	14.2	7.36	17.2
OAK	Oquist (R)	4:35	-145	4-3	5.13	6-8	1-0	7.2	2.35	2-0	19.0	5.68	11.8
At SEA	Swift (R)			6-4	4.54	6-7	0-0	0.0	0.00	1-1	15.1	1.17	11.2
NY	Irabu (R)	8:05	-120	6-2	1.68	7-4	0-0	0.0	0.00	2-1	20.1	2.21	11.1
At CLE	Colon (R)			6-4	2.73	7-7	0-0	0.0	0.00	2-1	25.2	1.40	7.0
TEX	Perisho (L)	8:05	-140	0-1	23.14	0-1	0-0	0.0	0.00	2-1	21.0	3.00	10.3
At ANA	Dickson (R)			7-4	5.43	9-4	0-0	0.0	0.00	3-0			30.9
NATIONAL LEAGUE													
ATL	Neagle (L)	1:35	-170	8-4	3.18	10-5	1-0	7.0	1.29	1-2	24.0	3.75	9.0
At MON	Hermanson (R)			4-6	3.20	4-7	0-0	0.0	0.00	1-2	17.0	1.59	10.6
FLA	Fontenot (R)	1:40	-350	0-4	8.14	0-5	0-0	0.0	0.00	0-2	17.0	6.35	16.9
At NY	Leiter (L)			8-3	1.53	8-5	0-0	0.0	0.00	3-0	21.0	0.86	9.0
PIT	Loaiza (R)	2:05	-150	4-3	4.73	4-6	0-0	0.1	0.00	1-2	17.0	4.24	14.3
At MIL	Juden (R)			6-5	4.08	7-8	1-0	13.0	0.69	1-1	19.0	4.26	11.8
ARI	Daal (L)	2:10	-150	3-4	2.82	5-3	0-0	0.0	0.00	2-1	23.0	2.74	10.6
At St. L	Acevedo (R)			2-1	4.68	2-2	0-0	2.0	9.00	1-0	13.0	4.85	11.8
PHI	Green (R)	2:20	-165	4-4	5.21	5-8	0-0	0.0	0.00	1-0	18.2	6.27	14.0
At CHI	Trachsel(R)			6-3	4.04	8-6	0-0	0.0	0.00	0-2	19.2	6.41	13.7
CIN	Harnisch (R)	2:35	-130	6-2	2.78	7-8	0-0	0.0	0.00	1-1	21.0	1.71	9.4
At HOU	Schourek (L)			3-5	4.70	3-5	0-0	0.0	0.00	1-2	17.0	4.24	11.6
LA	Park (R)	3:05	-110	5-4	4.63	8-7	0-0	0.0	0.00	1-1	21.0	3.43	10.7
At COL	Jones (R)			1-2	5.55	3-2	0-0	0.0	0.00	0-2	17.0	7.41	16.9
SD	Brown (R)	4:05	-120	7-3	2.84	10-6	0-0	0.0	0.00	2-0	20.0	4.50	14.0
At SF	Hershiser (R)			6-4	3.27	10-5	0-0	0.0	0.00	1-1	16.1	4.96	17.6

KEY: TEAM REC – Team's record in games started by today's pitcher. AHWG – Average hits and walks allowed per game in last 3 starts.

baseball game. The next two columns show the pitchers' performance up to that point in the season. W-L indicates the pitchers' record (wins and losses), and ERA indicates their earned run averages (ERA is basically the number of runs the pitcher is yielding on average in a 9-inning game). The rest of the columns provide information about each team's record when the pitcher starts the game, the pitcher's success (or failure) against the opponent this year, the pitcher's performance in his last three starts, and (for the number-crunching rotisserie baseball fans) the average number of hits and walks the pitcher has yielded per 9 innings in his last three starts. The acronym for this statistic – AHWG – is surprisingly similar to the sound a pitcher makes after giving up a home run.

Yankee Stadium Promotions

The Yankees also offer special promotions throughout the year, mostly targeted at younger fans (This means complimentary souvenirs!). Popular promotions include Beanie Babies Day, Cap Day, Batting Helmet Bank Day, and Tote Bag Day. Call the Yankees Ticket Office for more information (see Ordering Tickets section)

Ordering Tickets

Yankees Clubhouse Stores

You can buy your Yankees tickets from any of five Yankees Clubhouse Stores: In Manhattan: 110 E. 59th Street, between Lexington and Park, (212) 758-7844; 393 Fifth Ave, between 36th and 37th Streets, (212) 685-4693; 8 Fulton Street, (212) 514-7182: 245 West 42nd Street, between 7th and 8th Ave, (212) 768-9555. In White Plains: The Galleria, 100 Main Street, (919) 328-4272. These stores do not accept telephone orders, so you must buy your tickets in person.

Tickets By Phone

For ticket availability and to purchase tickets, call Ticket Master at any of the following phone numbers: (212) 307-1212, (201) 507-8900, (518) 476-1000, (914) 454-3388, (860) 525-4500, (609) 520-8383, (631) 888-9000, (203) 624-0033, (203) 744-8100. You will pay a $3 shipping and handling charge for the entire order, and if you are ordering at least 9 days in advance, they will mail the tickets to you. Otherwise, you'll have to pick up your tickets before the game at the Paid Reservation Window next to Gate 4.

Cyber-Tickets

The easiest way to purchase Yankee tickets is through their website at www.yankees.com. Check out their Stadium Seating Viewer, which gives you photo-like views of the field from various sections throughout the stadium.

Advanced Ticket Window

Tickets can also be purchased at the Advanced Ticket Windows located outside, adjacent from Gate 4 and parking lot 8, and inside the Stadium at section 9 until the end of the 7th inning. Starting March 1st, the Advanced Ticket Window is open Mon - Sat 9 - 5 P.M., and Sunday 10 - 4 P.M.

Discounted Ticket Programs

The Yankees offer special ticket programs throughout the year, such as Senior citizen games ($2 tickets), student-teacher games (half price), Tuesday Night Out games ($9), youth and family games, and free tickets for active military personnel. Contact the Yankees at (718) 293-6000 for more information.

Group Tickets

If you're able to organize a large group to attend a game (25 or more fans), you should contact the Yankees about a group package (718-293-6013). Your group will receive 2 bonus tickets for every 25 paid tickets, preferred seating, and your group's name in lights on the Stadium's centerfield message board.

Yankee Stadium Ticket Exchange Policy

The Yankees do not allow you to exchange your ticket, with the exception of rain-outs. If your game is rained-out, you will be allowed to exchange your ticket for the same priced seat either at the rescheduled game or any other Yankees home game within 12 months of the rained-out game. Exchanges can be made at Yankee Stadium or by mail (NY Ticket Office, Yankee Stadium, Bronx, NY 10451).

Early Bird Tip!

Once the playoffs end, it is time to start thinking about next season's tickets! For regular season tickets, the Yankees usually announce that tickets will go on sale in early December.

Guided Tours

Guided tours are available year-round. Generally tours are Monday through Saturday at 12:00 noon. For groups of 12 or more, reservations are required. During the season (April through October) and when the team is in town, limited tours are available and clubhouse access is restricted. The cost for a Yankee Stadium tour is $8 for adults and $4 for children (14 and under) and senior citizens. If you have any questions regarding the tours, or would like to make a group reservation, call (718) 579-4531.

Buying From Scalpers

A trained eye can pick them out of the crowd. crowd. They almost always have an obnoxious, impatient expression and a snake-like demeanor. No, I'm not referring to Mets fans. I'm talking about scalpers.

Benefits to buying from Scalpers

- If you're one of those people who like to negotiate and "win" all the time, buying from scalpers might just be your next hobby.

- If you're going to a game that isn't that popular, you can often get a good deal right before game-time from scalpers looking to unload their inventory. Also, if you're willing to miss a little bit of the action, you can get really good deals (often face value or below) by buying the tickets after the game has started.

- Breaking the law can be an exhilarating experience.

Hazards of buying from Scalpers

• Because you're waiting until game-time to buy your tickets (as opposed to buying in advance from the team, a ticket agency, or a broker), you have the stress of not knowing if you have tickets until the very last minute.

• You run the risk of getting lousy seats and/or not getting tickets at all (depending on how big the game is).

• Because the transaction occurs on a street corner, and is usually rushed, you don't have the time (or usually a seating diagram) to really understand where your seats are. So you run the risk of getting supposedly "really good seats" that actually aren't so good.

• On rare occasions, you might get conned by someone and get tickets that aren't quite legit. This is pretty unusual, however.

• You might end up in the slammer.

Picking the Best
Place to Sit

While it is hard to find a bad seat anywhere in Yankee Stadium, here are some guidelines that will help you get the best seat possible. First, it is important to understand how the stadium seating is organized. There are 5 major groups of seats: the bleachers (behind the outfield), the Tier level (upper deck), the Loge level (middle deck), the Main level (lower level), and Field Boxes (closest to the field). **With the exception of the bleachers, the sections are numbered in such a way that odd numbered sections are located along the first base and right field side, and even numbered sections are located along the third base and left field side of the field.** This makes it pretty easy for you to figure out where you're sitting just by looking at the section number on your ticket.

Also, it is important to know what kind of a view you'll be getting when you buy your tickets. For all non-bleacher sections, the view from your seats will fall into one of four categories: (a) "home plate views," (b) "infield views," (c) "neck-benders," and (d) "outfield views." "Home plate views" put you right behind home plate, which is great if you like to watch the pitcher-hitter confrontation. The downside is that you are likely to watch the game through a protective net, since hitters often foul off pitches directly behind home plate. "Infield views" are probably the best view of all, because it gives you a great view of the entire infield and outfield, and is a good spot to snare foul balls. "Neck-bender" seats are named because fans sitting too far past first or third bases must turn their head to the left or right to follow the action at home plate. After a few hours of turning your neck 90 degrees, you may want to schedule an appointment with your chiropractor. Finally, "outfield views" are located past either foul pole in the outfield. While these seats are the farthest away, they are angled nicely towards the infield diamond, unlike the "neck-bender" seats.

Bleachers

$8 / $10 – Perhaps the most jovial section of Yankee Stadium, it is mostly populated by young, rowdy fans interested in harassing opposing pitchers (in the bullpen) and opposing outfielders. These seats are the farthest from home plate (and thus farthest from the majority of the action), but fans enjoy this section for its fun-loving atmosphere and panoramic view of Yankee Stadium. The bleachers are great on warm summer days, but because there is no shade, be sure to bring some sunscreen. If rain is a possibility, remember that you will be completely exposed to the elements.

The bleachers are split into two parts, one group of seats behind left-centerfield, and another group of seats behind right field. The center portion of the bleachers was covered to provide hitters with a better hitting background. The left side of the bleachers – called the "second bleachers section" – is further from home plate than the right side, because Monument Park and the bullpens separate this

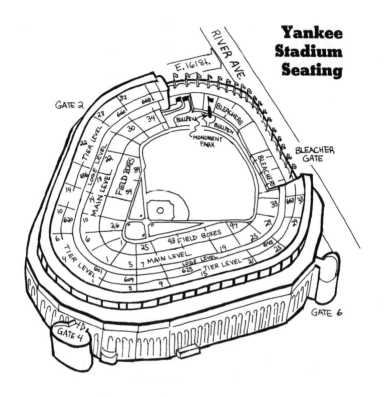

Yankee Stadium Seating

part of the bleachers from the outfield. Despite the presence of the monuments and the bullpens, fans still have an unobstructed view of the field. The seats in this section, however, are not always sold, but are usually made available on special days, for special groups, or if the game is a complete sellout. The right side of the bleachers (sections

37-43) is closer to homeplate, and is home to the "bleacher creatures" a group of fans known for their extreme rowdiness and loyalty to the Yankees.

There are some drawbacks to sitting in the bleachers. First, you won't have a great view of the Stadium's main scoreboard (which resides behind and above the bleachers), although fans in the bleachers can follow the game by viewing the auxiliary scoreboards above first and third bases. Second, the bleachers section – true to its name – contains steel benches, so if you're looking for a comfortable seat with a seat-back, this is the wrong section for you. Third, the seats are not reserved, so you'll have to fend for yourself in finding a spot to sit. Finally, the bleachers are isolated from the rest of the Stadium, so if you want to walk around and take in the many angles of Yankee Stadium, you'll find the bleachers too confining. You also will be restricted from entering Monument Park prior to the game. Of course, you can't beat the price!

Tier Reserved Seats

$18 / $20 – The highest possible spot to sit in at Yankee Stadium, these seats offer unobstructed views of the entire field. Also, you'll be completely exposed to the elements.

Home plate views: sections 1-8
Infield views: sections 9- 20
Neck bender views: sections 21 - 30
Outfield views: sections 31 - 36

Tier Box Seats

$33 / $35 – This section is the lower portion of the upper deck. Because you're paying significantly more than the Tier Reserved seats, you should make sure you're getting a seat that's in one of the lower rows in the section. Otherwise it's a better deal to buy a ticket in the Tier Reserved section, which may only be a few rows higher. Like the Tier Reserved seats, you'll be exposed to the elements.

Home plate views: sections 601- 616
Infield views: sections 617 - 640
Neck bender views: sections 641 - 660
Outfield views: sections 661 - 670

Loge Box Seats

$40 / $45 – The Loge level offers a great view of the action, as it is closer to the field than the Tier level. This section is pretty much sheltered by the Tier Level seating, so you won't get much sun sitting in this area. You'll stay dry, however, if it drizzles.

Home plate views: not available to the public
Infield views: sections 419 - 472
Neck bender views: sections 473 - 519
Outfield views: sections 519 - 548

Main Reserved Seats

$35 / $40 – The Reserved section is the closest you can get to the field without sitting in a box seat. You'll be close to the action, but because this section is located below the loge level you won't get much sun.

Home plate views: sections 1 - 8
Infield views: sections 9 - 18
Neck bender views: sections 19 - 30
Outfield views: sections 31 - 36

Main Box Seats

$45 / $50 – This section gets you close to the field and enables you to enjoy the outdoors without sitting in the shadow of the loge and tier levels above.

Home plate views: sections 201 - 228
Infield views: sections 229 - 286
Neck bender views: sections 287 - 330
Outfield views: sections 331 - 350

Field Box Seats

$50 / $55 – These seats are the closest to the field, and give you a chance to really experience the sights and sounds of the game. Of course, if you can't get these seats you can always sneak down to this section in the late innings of a game.

Home plate views: Not Available to the Public
Infield views: Not Available to the Public
Neck bender views: sections 81 - 118
Outfield views: sections 119 - 136

Standing Room Only

The Yankees do not have a standing room only area.

Alcohol-Free Sections

For those of you who would like to sit in an alcohol-free zone, buy your tickets in sections 29, 31, 33, or 35 on the Loge Level, or in sections 8 and 9 on the Tier Reserved Level.

Handicapped Seating and Access

Yankee Stadium offers seating specifically designed for wheelchairs. These sections are located on the field level, rows K, Boxes 1-12. Also, seating is available in Reserved sections 2, 7, 8, and 10. Handicapped elevators are located in Sections 15 and 22.

How to Drive to Yankee Stadium

Driving to Yankee Stadium is pretty simple. Yankee Stadium is located in the Bronx at 161st St. and River Ave. If you're driving northbound on I-87, take exit 4 (149th St.) or exit 5 (155th St.) Driving southbound on I-87, take exit 6 (161st St). Once you've exited you'll see signs to the Stadium.

Parking Guide

Your best option is to park in any of the Kinney Parking Lots, which are scattered around Yankee Stadium. These lots cost $6 and allow you to park your car without fear of it being boxed-in, vandalized, or stolen. The latest time to pick up your car is 2 hours after the final pitch of the game. You will find Kinney Lots in the following locations (please see parking map), along with star ratings indicating how close the lots are to the stadium:

1. River Ave. at 71 E. 153rd St. (handicapped parking available)

2. River Ave – East 158th St. & East 157th St.

3. East 157th St. – River Ave. & Gerard Ave.

4. River Ave. – East 157th St. & 153rd St. (valet parking available)

★★

5. East 153rd St. at River Ave.

6. Exterior St. at Market Area

7. East 161 St. – Jerome Ave. & Macombs Dam Bridge

★

8. Jerome Ave. – East 164 St. & East 162nd St.

9. River Ave. at East 151st St.

10. River Ave. – East 151st St. & East 150th St. (2 locations)

11. River Ave. – East 164th St. & East 165th St. (Bus lot)

Rating Key

★★★ Yankee Stadium connoisseur's choice

★★ Seasoned Yankee fan's pick

★ Only under extreme time duress

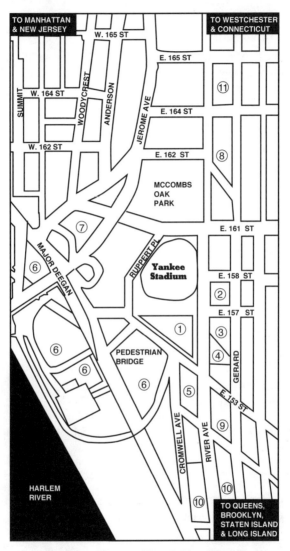

Yankee Fan's Parking Guide

Alternatives to Driving

If you don't want to deal with the hassle of driving (or if you're an ardent environmentalist), you have three alternatives to driving.

Subway

If you don't mind taking the subway, you can get to Yankee Stadium on several different subway lines. A trip from downtown Manhattan takes less than 25 minutes. The Yankee Stadium subway stop is located right outside the Stadium at the corner of 161st St. and River Ave. The #4 train (east side) as well as the B (west side weekdays only) and D trains (west side) make stops at 161st St./Yankee Stadium. Metro North train service to Connecticut and Westchester County is available at the 125 St. subway stop.

SUBWAY MAP

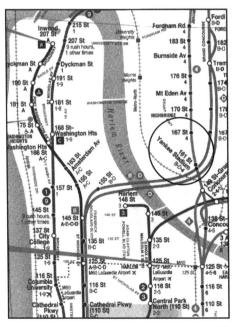

Buses

Several New York City Transit Authority Bus Lines provide convenient service to Yankee Stadium. The BX 6, BX 13, and BX 55 buses stop at 161st St./Yankee Stadium. Also, the BX 1 bus stops at 161st St./Grand Concourse, a short walk from the Stadium. For more information on subway and bus transportation to Yankee Stadium, contact the NYC Transit Authority at (718) 330-1234 between 6am and 9pm.

Ferry

If traveling by sea is your thing, you can take a ferry from Manhattan or New Jersey to Yankee Stadium. For information and ferry schedule, call 1-800-53-FERRY in Manhattan or 1-800-BOAT-RIDE.

What to Bring

Observe the weather conditions, dress appropriately, and bring the necessary extras such as a windbreaker for windy, colder weather, an umbrella in case of rain, and sunscreen on sunny days. Sporting white and blue garments will reinforce your Yankees loyalty, as will wearing a Yankees hat or T-shirt. Since you will most likely be sitting in the "common-man" areas, don't wear expensive, silk garments, because spilled bear or mustard are facts of life at any ball park. Small children and infants should be wrapped in swaddling Yankees colors. Sun-glasses (and regular glasses) are a plus, as are opera glasses or binoculars. You are allowed to bring a camera, so if it's convenient, bring it and capture Yankee Stadium's colorful charm. Be careful about bringing too many things, however, as there is very little room in front of and under your seat. One last thing... make sure to bring this guide!

What Not to Bring

First, avoid wearing hats and/or paraphernalia from other baseball teams (especially the Red Sox). Harmless as it may seem, you risk being harassed by Yankee fans in your section. Also, there are several items which Yankees security will not allow you to enter with: cans, bottles (glass or plastic), jugs, coolers, or hard containers of any kind. Furthermore, due to increased security measures, backpacks and any other large bags are not permitted in the stadium.

Rules on Banners and Signs

I f you want to bring a sign or banner to the game, make sure that you don't hang it in any part of fair territory, or obstruct the views of other fans (even Red Sox fans). Also, you will not be allowed to parade through the general seating areas between innings with your sign. Finally, your banner will be confiscated if you use any kind of weight to keep it in place.

CHAPTER TWO

PLAY BALL!

Pre-Game Activities

On radio station WABC 770 AM, there is a pre-game show 30 minutes before the game, with players and the Yankees manager interviewed in the show. Tailgate barbecuing is not an option because you will most likely be parked in tightly with other cars and won't have room for a barbecue (save this for a Giants or Jets game!) If you want to have a snack, a drink, or a meal before the game, here are some suggestions:

Eat in the Park

The absolute best pre-game activity is getting into the park early, munching on some Yankee Franks, and taking in batting practice. The food inside the park is decent, and reasonably priced. Besides, the true baseball fan eats ball park food, not fancy restaurant cuisine!

If you don't want to eat in the park and decide to pass on the many outdoor food vendors, here are a few recommended eateries surrounding the Stadium:

Sidewalk Café

Located just outside the stadium between Gates 4 and 6, this enclosed area is a nice place to have a bite to eat. The café opens at 11 am on day games, and 5pm on night games.

Billy's Stadium Sport Bar

Located on River Ave. across the street from the Stadium. Sports Bar with typical sports bar food.

Stan's Sports Bar and Restaurant

Also located on River Ave. Typical sports bar food.

Ball Park Sports Bar & Grill

Located further down River Ave. Sports bar food combined with a souvenir shop and bowling lanes.

Yankee Tavern Food & Drink

Located about a block from the Stadium at the corner of E. 161st and Gerard. A fun place to eat before or after the game. Lots of Yankee memorabilia such as photographs of Yankee greats, and big, colorful murals of stars such as Ruth, Gehrig, and DiMaggio.

Yankee Pizza

Located on E. 161st between Gerard and Walton. A small pizza shop with decent pizza and calzones.

Court Deli Restaurant

Located at the corner of E. 161st and Walton. A typical NY Deli.

Monument Park

No trip to Yankee Stadium is complete without a pre-game visit to Monument Park (see Characteristics of Yankee Stadium, page 58). Monument Park, located behind the left field fence, contains stone plaques dedicated to former Yankee greats such as Babe Ruth, Lou Gehrig, and Joe DiMaggio. Monument Park is open from the time the Stadium gates open, and up until 45 minutes prior to game time. To visit Monument Park, go to section 36 between the Field and Main Level seats, and take the staircase to Monument Park.

Getting into the Stadium

"Whew, I thought we would have to call in the fire department, my team's so hot." – Casey Stengel, after his NY Mets snapped a 17-game losing streak.

You can enter the park up to an hour and a half before game time (Monday through Friday) and up to 2 hours prior to game time on Saturdays, Sundays and holidays.

If you're sitting in the bleachers, the Stadium entrance is located on River Ave. For fans sitting along the third base line of the Stadium, enter through Gate 2 on 161st Street. For fans sitting behind home plate or along the first base side  of the Stadium, enter through Gates 4 and 6 which are located on 157th and Rupert Streets. See stadium map on page 26.

Taking Care of the One You Love — Your Stomach

Find your seat first — then get your food. There is nothing worse than staggering through crowded Sections of the park, arms full of teetering sodas and food, with your ticket in your mouth, trying to find your row ("excuse me, pardon me..."). It is also unpleasant for the other people you are disturbing.

There are food concession stands scattered throughout the Main, Field, Loge, and Tier levels, which offer the standard ballpark menu (beer, soda, hot dogs, pretzels, and other snacks). If you're looking for more variety, you can seek out the following concession stands: If you're sitting in the main or field level, you will find a food court (similar to standard ballpark menu but also offers specialty sausage, TCBY Yogurt, deli sandwiches, pizza, hamburgers, cheeseburgers, french fries, chicken fingers, nachos, and imported beer) along the left field side of the Stadium. You will also find a pasta and pizza stand, a soft ice cream stand, and a specialty sausage stand along the right side of the Stadium behind the Yankees dugout. Also, on the Tier level you will find, in addition to the many standard menu concession stands, an imported beer stand behind home plate. You will also find a stand behind the visitor's dugout that offers chicken fingers, hot dogs, sausage, hamburgers, french fries, and soda and beer.

Yankee Stadium Beer Rules

If you like to drink a few beers during a ball game, you should become familiar with "the beer rules." Study them, commit them to memory, for they shall govern your consumption at Yankee stadium.

Rule 1: Thou Shalt buy only two beers at a time in the bleachers.

Rule 2: Thou Shalt not buy a beer without identification.

Rule 3 Thou Shalt not buy beer at the start of the 7th inning or two hours into the game.

Rule 4: Thou Shalt not drink beer in Sections 8 and 9.

Rule 5: Thou Shalt not consume too much beer and be removed by security.

General Information

Telephones
Located on each side of the Stadium, and on every level

Men's/Ladies' Rooms
Located on each side of the Stadium, and on every level

Customer Service Booths
Located on the Field Level behind Sections 2,9, and 33; on the Main Level behind Section 3; on the Loge Level behind Section 7; on the Tier Level behind Section 4.

Souvenir Stands
Six souvenir stands and two gift shops are located throughout the main and field levels. On the Loge Level there are four souvenir stands, but no gift shops. On the Tier level, there is one souvenir stand behind home plate.

Designated Driver Booth
If you volunteer to be your group's designated driver, go to section 4 on the Field Level and you'll receive coupons for free sodas!

First Aid
Located in Section 2 on the Field Level, and in Section 15 on the Main Level.

Lost and Found
Located in the Yankee executive office behind home plate.

ATMs
Two ATMs are located along the right side of the Stadium (section 9 behind the Yankee dugout) and along the left side of the Stadium (section 20 in shallow left field).

Following the Game

During the course of a game you will discover several areas of the stadium which provide information on player statistics, the score of the game, the scores of other games in progress, and the current number of balls, strikes, and outs.

There are two auxiliary scoreboards above first and third bases. The illustration below shows these scoreboards during a game between the Yankees and Indians. The scoreboards show the number of runs scored by each team, the number of the player currently batting, balls, strikes, outs, and the inning.

CLE	NY	AT BAT	BALLS	STRIKES	OUT	INN
2	5	42	3	1	1	7

Three main scoreboards, located in center and right fields behind the bleachers, show the scoring by inning, as well as player statistics and Diamond Vision replays.

Characteristics of Yankee Stadium

Dimensions

Yankee Stadium's dimensions are 314 feet to the right field foul pole, 385 feet to right center, 408 feet to to center field, 399 feet to left center, and 318 feet to the left field foul pole. These current dimensions are radically different than those of "Old Yankee Stadium." Prior to the 1976 renovation, the left and right field foul poles were much closer (301 feet and 296 feet respectively), while the outfield dimensions were much greater. Most notably, "Old Yankee Stadium" featured very deep center field and left-center field dimensions of 457 feet and 461 feet respectively. Deep left and center fields were nicknamed "Death Valley" as many sluggers watched in dismay as their well-struck drives died there.

Another current Yankee Stadium quirk is the asymmetrical dimensions of the outfield fence, which is 8 feet high in left field, 7 feet high in left-center and center fields, 9 feet high in right-center field, and 10 feet high in right field. The Yankees claim that the fence is designed correctly, but that the field slopes and causes the fence to have various heights.

Architectural Touches

Yankee Stadium's cathedral windows on the outside give the Stadium a cathedral-like quality. This is consistent with the notion that witnessing a game at Yankee Stadium is indeed a religious experience. The beautiful arched art-deco frieze, which originally resided along the stadium roof facade, was removed but a portion hangs above the center field bleachers.

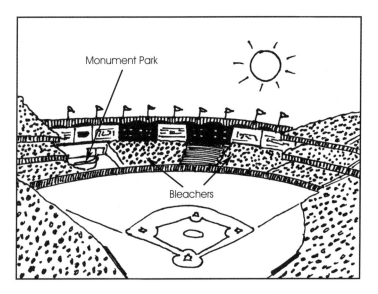

The Bat

Located outside in front of Yankee Stadium, this 120 foot high boiler stack has a unique flair to it. If you look closely at it you will make out the resemblance to an upside-down baseball bat. In fact, the smokestack has been modified to look just like a gigantic Louisville Slugger bat, including the manufacturer's seal and the Babe's signature.

Right Field Bleachers

The right field bleachers are as integral to Yankee Stadium's history as any other part of the ball park. Back in the 20's and 30's the bleachers were nicknamed "Ruthville" and "Gehrigville," due to the sluggers' propensity to hit titanic home runs into the crowd of crazed bleacher fans. The once enormous right field bleachers section has changed over the years, and now has a concrete base (vs. wooden) and is much smaller in size.

Bullpens

Located in left field, these bullpens have seen some of the greatest pitchers in baseball history warm up their golden arms. Legend has it that Yankee starting pitcher Whitey Ford would arrange for a table with a full-course dinner to arrive in the bullpen. The ever confident Ford explained that since his fellow relievers would not be getting any work during the game (he assumed, of course, that he would pitch the entire 9 innings), they should at least enjoy themselves.

Monument Park

Monument Park honors great Yankees players and managers. A virtual museum of Yankees history, Monument Park allows fans to view the three original stone monuments of Ruth, Huggins, and Gehrig, as well as a fourth which was added to honor Mickey Mantle. Numerous plaques have been added to honor Ed Barrow (early general manager who converted Ruth from a pitcher into an outfielder), Jacob Ruppert (the great Yankee owner who started the club's dynasty), Joe DiMaggio, Casey Stengel, Joe McCarthy, Pope Paul VI, Thurman Munson, Pope John Paul II, Billy Martin, Whitey Ford, Left Gomez, Roger Maris, Allie Reynolds, Elston Howard, Phil Rizzuto, Bill Dickey, and Yogi Berra. Do not leave Yankee Stadium without visiting this special place.

Yankee Fans

Adjectives often used to describe Yankee fans are: insane, knowledgeable, partisan, scary, vulgar, ruthless. Your Yankee Stadium experience is incomplete until you see, hear, feel, and perhaps even smell the will of Yankee fans. During a Yankee rally, the fans will cheer until the rafters shake, stomp their feet in the bleachers, and generally rock "The House That Ruth Built." People drawing the ire of Yankee fans include visiting players, umpires who have the gaul to make calls against the home team, and visiting fans stupid enough to wear their team paraphernalia (particularly Boston fans). The hair-raising scenario of Yankee Stadium promoting "Bat Night" (during which the first 30,000 or so fans receive a free bat) has actually occurred. Yankee fans are bad enough without weapons. Perhaps Yankee Stadium should have a "Hand-cuff Night" or "Sedative Night" instead.

Famous Spots

Right Field Bleachers

Three historically-important home run balls have landed in the right field bleachers. The first occurred on September 30th, the last day of the 1927 season, when Babe Ruth hit his 60th home run of the season. The ball landed in the first row in the right field bleachers, just fair. The record 60th home run would stand for 34 years.

The second home run occurred on October 1st, 1961, when Roger Maris broke one of baseball's sacred records. Maris took Red Sox pitcher Tracey Stallard's offering and launched it into box 163D of right field's section 33. Maris' 61st home run was controversial for several reasons. First, many fans did not deem Maris worthy of breaking Ruth's record, and would have preferred Maris' more popular teammate Mickey Mantle to break the mark. Second, Maris' home run record would become saddled with the dreaded "asterisk," since his 61 homeruns had been hit in 162 games versus Ruth's 154 games.

The third home run occurred 2 years later on May 22, 1963. On a pitch from Kansas City's Bill Fischer, Mickey Mantle rocketed the ball high in the air and off the right field facade. Had the ball been hit just 6 inches higher, it would have cleared the roof and traveled an estimated 620 feet. It also would have been the only fair ball ever hit out of Yankee Stadium.

Infield

Of the many player appreciation days in Yankee Stadium history, none were as poignant as Lou Gehrig Appreciation Day on July 4, 1939. Surrounded by 62,000 fans and by players from the Murder's Row team of 1927, Gehrig gave his "luckiest man on the face of the earth" speech. Gehrig died two years later from amyotrophic lateral sclerosis, now known as "Lou Gehrig's Disease."

Pitchers Mound

The pitchers mound in Yankee stadium has witnessed eight Yankee hurlers pitch no-hitters. In 1938, Monte Pearson no-hit Cleveland, followed by Allie Reynold's blanking of Boston in 1951. Perhaps the most dramatic no-hitter was thrown on October 8, 1956, by Don Larsen, who beat Brooklyn in the World Series with a perfect game (not hits and no walks). Yankee no-hitters returned in the 80's as Dave Righetti no-hit the Red Sox in July of 1983. Four Yankee no-hitters occurred in the 90's, as the one-armed Jim Abbott (1993), Dwight Gooden (1996), David Wells (1998), and David Cone (1999) turned the trick.

Home Plate

No discussion of famous spots in Yankee
Stadium would be complete without mentioning
home plate. Of course, Ruth's 60th and Maris'
61st homeruns qualify. Joe DiMaggio's 56 game hitting
streak began at homeplate in May of 1941. Perhaps the
most spectacular performance at the plate occurred during the 1977 World Series, as Reggie Jackson hit three consecutive homeruns on three pitches from three different Los
Angeles Dodgers pitchers. Mr. October's homeruns helped
the Yankees win their first world championship since 1962.

Outfield

Three of baseball's greatest players patrolled the outfield for
the Yankees. With Babe Ruth in right field, and Joe
DiMaggio and Mickey Mantle in center field, the Yankees
had at least one Hall-of-Fame outfielder in their outfield for
almost five consecutive decades.

Yankee Stadium Favorites

Yankee Stadium Sights

- Walking from the far corner of left field (next to Monument Park) to the far corner of right field. Taking in the various vantage points of the game as you work your way to right field.

- Participating in the "Wave," which usually starts in the bleachers, and almost always travels clockwise through the bleachers, into right field, and on through to left field.

- Watching the manager and the umpire arguing, escalating to the point where both are less than an inch apart, spraying saliva on each others faces, and always yelling at the same time.

- Watching the cleaning crew primp and preen the infield dirt and mound between the 5th and 6th innings and dance to the song "YMCA".

- Watching beach balls ricochet around the bleachers, or even better, being in the bleachers and striking one of the balls.

- Watching the grounds crew covering the field during a rain delay.

- Witnessing the crowd's and players' reaction to a squirrel or a rat racing across the outfield.

- Watching "Freddy", the unofficial mascot of the Yankees, who wanders throughout the stands and gives fans a chance to ring a metal pot that hangs around his neck.

Yankee Stadium Sounds and Smells

- The home plate umpire howling or grunting a called third strike on a bewildered batter.

- The crescendo of the crowd cheering as a well struck ball rises majestically over the outfield fence and into the bleachers for a home run.

- The National Anthem, and "Take Me Out to the Ball game" (sung during the 7th inning stretch).

- The combination of mustard, hot dogs, fresh air, cigar smoke, bubble gum, and roasted peanuts: a unique scent only found in baseball parks.

- The smell of the leather of a baseball glove that you've brought to track down foul balls.

- The smell of sizzling sausages outside of Yankee Stadium at the vendor carts.

- Hearing Yankees radio announcer John Sterling, at the end of every Yankees win, yelling "The Yankees win! Thhhheeeeeeeee Yankees win!".

- The sound of Frank Sinatra's "New York, New York", played after each Yankees win.

Talk Like a Fan

"Whenever I decided to release a guy, I always had his room searched first for a gun. You couldn't take any chances with some of those birds." – Casey Stengel

If you really want to be part of the "Yankee Stadium faithful," you need to master the slang, the delivery, the attitude of a true Yankee fan. The basic idea is to be wildly biased towards the Yankees, wildly opposed to the other team, and fickle with the umpires. Booing should be reserved for members of the other team, and only under extreme conditions is it acceptable to lay your wrath on a Yankee player. Extreme condition example: The Yankee clean-up hitter has not hit a home run in 2 months, is hitting below .200, has stranded 6 runners in the game thus far, and has just struck out with the bases loaded with the Yankees down by 2 runs.

Slang

Mastering Yankee Stadium fanhood starts with a thorough knowledge of baseball slang. Your correct usage of words and expressions will allow you to feel at home with the established "Yankee Stadium Faithful" in your section.

Talk like a New Yawk-uh

Yankee Stadium fanhood also involves mastery of the New York accent, which can take years of practice to imitate properly. A realistic first step is to learn how to decode the commentary you'll hear hear from the surrounding Yankee fans. Here are some examples:

"When Moosina troes da slidah, fugheddaboudit. The hitta just says "whatevuh" 'cause he knows he can't hit it."

– Yankee fan commenting on the pitching prowess of Yankee ace Mike Mussina.

"If Steinbrenna trades faw anutha closuh, noo yawk il win a-nutha champ-yin-chip fa shoowa."

– Yankee fan anticipating a key trade by Yankees Owner George Steinbrenner.

"Yaw pichin' like a little goil, Williams! This is noo yawk, Williams, and you can't pich like dat he-uh. That stuff may woyk in Baltimaw, but not he-uh in noo yawk! Hit the showiz, ya chump! Back to the min-iz!"

– Typical heckling of an opposing pitcher heard at Yankee Stadium.

"Jones yoos-da pich fawda Brewas a few yeaza-go. He hadda cuppa cawfee theah but he was traded to noo yawk last yeah."

– Yankee fan chronicling the recent career of a Yankees pitcher.

Yankee Stadium Slang for the Neophyte

Slang	What it Means	Secondary Meaning
Aspirin tablet	fastball	cure for hangover
Baltimore chop	weak hit chopped off front of plate	imitation of Atlanta fans
Banjo Hitter	poor contact, makes sick sound	musician at bat
Batting practice pitch	weak, easy-to-hit fastball	pitch thrown during practice
Beanball	pitch which hits the batter	edible pitch
Boot	fielding error	for illegally-parked car
Bridge Master	pitcher who allows too many homeruns	card-game genius
Brush back	pitch intentionally thrown close to batter	a shower activity
Bum	lousy player (used liberally for pitchers)	a person's underside
Bush league	lacking class (minor leaguer)	league for presidents
Cheese	fastball	edible mold
Chump	bum — used primarily for hitters	cousin of the chimpanzee
Comebacker	ball hit back at pitcher	boxer who keeps getting up
Cookie	an easy to hit pitch (see batting practice pitch)	a cute name for significant other
Cup of coffee	brief stint in majors with a team	morning drug
Dinger	homerun	hitting head on car door
Ducks on the pond	runners on base to be driven in	Central Park sight
Duster	brushback	household tool
Eephus pitch	10-12 feet in air, blooper pitch	no secondary meaning
Flake	eccentric player (pitcher)	dandruff
Gas	good fastball	result of a Yankee Stadium hot-dog
Green light	freedom to swing	signals chaos in New York traffic
Hanging curve	curve that doesn't break /easy to hit	your belly after too many beers

Slang	What it Means	Secondary Meaning
Head-hunting	throwing at batters' heads	the pigeons above
Hill	mound	Anita's last name
Homer	homerun	Simpsons character
Hook	curve	popular Peter Pan movie
Hot corner	3rd base	street corner in red-light district
Long-ball	also a homerun	book by Longfellow
Meatball	easy-to-hit pitch	Italian delicacy
Mop-up	pitch in relief way behind	janitor's duty
No-no	a no-hitter	words used by girlfriend
Ohfer	hitless day	grunting noise indicating pain
Out pitch	pitch a pitcher depends on to get batter out	no secondary meaning
Payoff pitch	full count pitch	illegally-funded pitch
Punch and Judy hitter	well placed soft singles	puppet who can hit
Purpose pitch	pitch thrown at batter to intimidate	politically-correct pitch
Quail shot (dying quail)	weak hit dropping in front of outfielders	Murphy Brown's comments
Scroogie	screwball pitch	Ebeneezer's nickname
Sitting duck	runner is picked off, thrown out easily	ugly duckling's lazy brother
Southpaw	left-handed pitcher	left-handed dog
Spitball	doctored (Vaseline pitch, pine tar ball)	seen flying off Eifel Tower
Stiff	lousy player (used mostly for batters)	your lower back in bleachers
Tater	homerun	an American dinner treat
Texas league single	lofted weakly into shallow outfield	no secondary meaning
Twin killing	double play	bizarre murder case
Uncle Charlie	curve ball	your father's brother
Wounded duck	weakly hit pop-up	hunter's nightmare
Yakker	sharp breaking curve	a good joke
Yellow yammer	curve	yellow bird

Games and Diversions

Let's face it. Sometimes a baseball game can be boring. Here are some games and diversions to get you through these slow moments

Mound game - A hat is rotated from person to person each half inning, at which time everyone puts in $1. At the end of the inning, players typically throw the baseball towards the pitcher's mound. If the ball lands on the mound (all dirt, no grass), the holder of the hat wins the pot. If the ball rolls off onto the grass, or never makes it to the mound, the hat is passed on to the next person and everyone adds another dollar to the hat.

Dollars - Start a hat with $1 from each person in your group. The hat is rotated every time a new batter steps to the plate. The holder of the hat wins money if the batter gets a hit ($1 for a single, $2 for a double, $3 for a triple, and the entire pot for a homerun). If the batter walks, is hit by a pitch, or reaches base by an error, the hat is passed on with no money added or withdrawn. If the batter makes an out, the holder of the hat has to put in $1. Double plays cost $2, and triple plays cost $3. Believe me, you'll never watch a ballgame closer than when you're playing Dollars!

Human Radar Gun – Watch the pitcher throw a pitch and guess the speed. Your friend watches the stadium radar gun (usually posted somewhere in the ball park) to see how close you are to the actual speed. If you get the speed exactly right, he pays you $5. If you're 1 MPH off, you pay him $1, 2 MPH off $2, and more than 2MPH off $3. After a few pitches you can actually get pretty good at this.

Keeping Score

"I remember one game I got five hits and stole five bases, but none of it was written down because they forgot to bring the scorebooks to the game that day." – Cool Papa Bell

Keeping score is one of baseball's great traditions, and has become a bit of a lost art. You'll mostly see old-timers enjoying this ancient ritual, but everyone should try it at least once. You can usually find a scorecard in the program that's sold at the ballpark, or you can use the scorecard provided on the following pages.

Your first step is to fill out some of the basics before the game starts, such as the teams, date, start time, etc. When the PA announcer gives you the starting lineup, you'll want to record each hitter (1 through 9), as well as note their position in the column entitled "Pos." Position numbers are assigned as follows: (1) pitcher; (2) catcher; (3) first baseman; (4) second baseman; (5) third baseman; (6) shortstop; (7) left fielder; (8) center fielder; (9) right fielder. Since pitchers don't hit in the American League, the pitcher (2) will be replaced in the lineup by the designated hitter (marked as DH).

When the Yankees are hitting, you'll be recording every major event that occurs in the innings. Let's consider a hypothetical inning, and see how we'd score it.

Lofton leads off the first inning of the game with a single to left center. Jeter, the second hitter, strikes out swinging. Rodriguez steps to the plate, and Lofton steals second base. Rodriguez ultimately walks. Giambi singles to left, scoring Lofton, and advancing Rodriguez to third. Posada makes his plate appearance, but unfortunately grounds into a double play, hitting it to the opposing shortstop, who flips it to the second baseman for the second out, who then throws it on to first for the third out.

Here is how the Yankees first inning would have been scored:

#	Player	Pos	1	2
7	Lofton	8	25 ⟋⟍ SB51 / 25 ⟍ 1B	◇
2	Jeter	6	① K	
13	Rodriguez	5	25 ◆ 25 / BB	◇
25	Giambi	3	② ⟋ 20	◇
20	Posada	2	DP 6-4-3 ③	◇

S	Runs	1	
U	Hits	2	
M	Errors	0	
S	Left on Base	2	

When the Yankees are pitching, scoring is a lot simpler. Just keep track of each Yankee pitchers totals in the space at the bottom of the scorecard.

How you score a baseball game is really up to you. Some fans simply mark an "X" if the batter makes a hit and an "O" if the batter is retired. Other fans record every detail, including the balls and strikes on each hitter. For those of you who want to go deep, here are some useful abbreviations:

1B — Single
2B — Double
3B — Triple
BB — Walk
HR — Homerun
E — Error
FC — Fielder's Choice
HBP — Hit by Pitch
I — Interference
IW — Intentional walk
F — Fly out
G — Ground Out
K — Strike out (swinging)
Ʞ — Strike out (looking)
FO — Foul Out
L — Line Out
SF — Sacrifice Fly
SH — Sacrifice Hit / Bunt
DP — Double Play
TP — Triple Play
U — Unassisted Put Out
CS — Caught Stealing
WP — Wild Pitch
PB — Passed Ball
BK — Balk

Baseball Scorecard

Team:			vs				
Date:			Start Time:				
Weather:							
Umpires:							

#	Player	Pos	1	2	3	4	5
	_____ sub		◇	◇	◇	◇	◇
	_____ sub		◇	◇	◇	◇	◇
	_____ sub		◇	◇	◇	◇	◇
	_____ sub		◇	◇	◇	◇	◇
	_____ sub		◇	◇	◇	◇	◇
	_____ sub		◇	◇	◇	◇	◇
	_____ sub		◇	◇	◇	◇	◇
	_____ sub		◇	◇	◇	◇	◇
	_____ sub		◇	◇	◇	◇	◇
	_____ sub		◇	◇	◇	◇	◇
	_____ sub		◇	◇	◇	◇	◇

S	Runs						
U	Hits						
M	Errors						
S	Left on Base						

Pitcher	W-L	IP	H	R	ER	BB

at									
End Time:				Time of Game:					
Scorer:									

6	7	8	9	10	AB	R	H	RBI	E
◇	◇	◇	◇	◇					
◇	◇	◇	◇	◇					
◇	◇	◇	◇	◇					
◇	◇	◇	◇	◇					
◇	◇	◇	◇	◇					
◇	◇	◇	◇	◇					
◇	◇	◇	◇	◇					
◇	◇	◇	◇	◇					
◇	◇	◇	◇	◇					
◇	◇	◇	◇	◇					
					TOTALS				
					AB:		RBI:		
					R:		E:		
					H:		LOB:		

SO	HB	BK	WP	TBF	Catcher				PB

Dealing with Managers, Umpires and Pitchers

Opposing Managers

As you become a Yankee Stadium fanatic you will find yourself disliking the opposing team's manager. Managers come in all different shapes, sizes, and personalities. Here are some basic categories that the other team's manager will likely fall into:

Ex-Player
- Fiery, wishes he could pick up a bat and take a swing.
- Prone to throwing Gatorade jugs onto the field in anger.
- Often yells at and kicks dirt onto the umpire.

Gambler
- Manages on gut feeling, "rolls the dice" frequently.
- Goes against conventional wisdom.

Computer Man
- Too analytical.
- Has all kinds of charts and numbers.

Text-book Manager
- Too theoretical.
- Manages from the old book.

Sleeping Beauty

- Sleeps in the dugout, drools.
- Wakes up to call the bull pen, or to make the long walk to the mound (sleep walking?).
- Usually over the age of 55.

Captain Hook

- Removes starting pitchers too early.
- Shows no patience with his pitchers.

Dealing with Umpires

"Many fans look upon an umpire as a necessary evil to the luxury of baseball, like the odor that follows an automobile." – Christy Mathewson

Cardinal rule: Take any call against the Yankees as a personal affront to your intelligence and integrity. Your goal is to sway the umpire's allegiance to that of the Yankees.

Common Tactics Used with Umpires

- On a call against the home team, yell "Get some glasses!" or "Get your prescription changed!"

- Cheer on the Yankees manager as he argues with the umpire.

- If the other manager argues, yell, "Kick him out, ump!"

- On close pitches called against the Yankees, groan or boo the ump, even if you are 100 feet away in the bleachers.

- If the opposing catcher goes to the mound to confer with his pitcher, groan, boo and yell at the ump to break it up.

Special Rules for Dealing with Pitchers

- If the Yankees relief pitcher is one strike away from ending the game, stand and clap rhythmically with the crowd in anticipation of the last out.

- When a Yankee relief pitcher comes out of the bull pen to finish the game, shower him with cheers to encourage him (you can even bow and pay homage). For pitchers  in the opposing team's bull pen, harass them and try to destroy their confidence. Relief pitchers are usually a mental wreck because they have to come into pressure-packed situations. They will always pretend they are cool and mean, but inside they're all frazzled.

- If any pitcher has a no-hitter (has not allowed any hits in the game), under no circumstances should you say the words "no-hitter" or directly acknowledge that the pitcher is doing this. It is bad luck, and will surely destroy the pitcher's karma.

Doing the Wave

1. Cheer it on to nurture it at the beginning.

2. Make sure to stand up, throw hands and arms up, and yell loud incoherent things.

3. The wave should only travel from left to right field and around clockwise.

4. Don't start the wave too early in the game — wait until slow moments in the middle innings.

Getting a Souvenir Ball

Catching a Foul Ball

There is perhaps no greater baseball game souvenir than a caught foul ball. In order to pull this off, you'll need a good dose of luck, and a healthy awareness of the fans sitting beside you who will undoubtedly try to snatch that ball from your grasp. Here are some "problem fans" to watch out for:

The helicopter – This fan's approach is to stick out his elbows and swing his torso rapidly from side to side, creating an immediate space between him and the other fans, and giving him a clean shot at catching the ball. Best Defense: An "accidental" splash of beer will slow those helicopter blades.

The Leach – (also known as "the jerk" or "the moocher") – This fan's strategy is to let YOU do all the work, and then snag the ball from you. After the ball caroms off your hands, arms, or face, he jumps into the action and steals the ball. A common variation of this move is to accidentally bump you while you're trying to catch the ball, which causes you to drop or bobble the ball. Once this occurs, it's a free for all and he's positioning down low to grab it off the ground. Best Defense: A pre-emptive "bump" while the ball is still in the air will give you the room you need to corral that ball.

The Child Robber – This low-life preys on the meek, waiting for a kid to catch the ball and then stealing it from him. Best Defense: Exposing this injustice to the rest of your section will transform the otherwise-friendly fans into an angry mob, who will take matters into their own hands.

The Pool Cleaner – This fan brandishes one of those long rods with a net on the end (the ones you'd use to clean your pool.) Because the rod is so long, this fan is able to "net" the ball in the air before it reaches anyone else. Best Defense: An even longer net.

Getting Players To Throw You a Ball

Another way to get a souvenir baseball is to simply ask for one. Here are some useful guidelines:

Things to yell to get a player to throw you a ball:

- "Hey Williams, can I have the ball?" – The straight-shooter approach.

- "Hey Williams, can I have the ball for my son?" – Works best if you do in fact have a son with you.

- "Hey Williams, I've only got four weeks to live, and it'd be a dream come true to have that ball." – Best used if you have some sort of bandage around your head.

- "Hey Williams, if you throw me a ball I'll let you autograph it for me late tonight at my apartment." – Works best if you're female, reasonably attractive, and scantily clothed.

Things NOT to yell if you want a player to throw you a ball:

- "Hey Johnson, throw me the %&##@ ball !" – Got his name wrong, too pushy, used profanity.

- "Hey Williams, you stink. You should be in the minors! Hey, can I have the ball?" – You clearly don't understand human relations.

- "Hey Williams, please please please please can I have a ball?" – Williams is likely to view you as pathetic, especially if you're an adult.

Post Game Tips

f you're not too tired after the game and are looking for some fun and food to occupy yourself while traffic dies down, here are some post-game suggestions:

Souvenirs

If you'd like to take some souvenirs home with you, you'll have plenty of options:

Stadium Souvenir Shops
Located behind section 24 near the food court, and behind section 23 next to the Sidewalk café, these shops offer an array of jerseys, hats, and other souvenirs.

Outdoor souvenir stands
These stands are scattered around the Stadium, and are a convenient but lower-quality alternative to the Stadium shops.

River Avenue Shops
A variety of shops scattered down River Ave. across from the Stadium (Stadium Souvenir, Stan's Sports World, Pro Cap Dugout, Stan the Man's Baseball Land, Ball Park Souvenirs).

Bowling

If you're so inclined, you can actually bowl a few frames at Ball Park Lanes, located on River Ave. across from the Stadium.

CHAPTER THREE

BASEBALL BASICS

Baseball 101

"You can observe a lot just by watching." – Yogi Berra

This basic introduction to baseball applies to the following types of fans:

- You are from another country (excluding Japan, Cuba, Dominican Republic, Taiwan, and Canada) and know nothing of baseball.

- You were raised by wolves and were recently discovered by scientists. You have just re-joined society and are trying to learn the culture.

- You recently sustained a blow to the head, and have long-term (and short-term) memory loss.

- You grew up in Milwaukee or Montreal and understandably don't know how the game is supposed to be played.

Regardless of your situation, you are forgiven, because you are taking steps to learn about America's pastime.

Basic Terminology

Baseball – The name of this game

Players – Grown men, dressed in pajama-like outfits, playing a game

Innings – Segments of a game. Baseball games aren't timed (unlike most sports) so a game ends when 9 innings are completed (unless the game is tied, which results in "extra innings").

Top and Bottom of an Inning – Each inning is divided into a top and bottom portion. The visiting team hits during the top of each inning, followed by the home team hitting in the bottom of the inning.

Strike zone – An invisible, square-shaped zone measuring from the batters knees to chest, and approximately 2 feet wide. The umpire behind the plate decides whether or not the ball is thrown for a "strike" (a ball passing through the zone) or a "ball" (thrown outside the strike zone).

Anatomy of a Team

A baseball team is comprised of the following types of players:

Pitcher – Stands on the pitchers mound and "pitches" the ball towards the batter. His job, generally speaking, is to make the hitter look foolish.

Hitter – Stands in the batters box at home plate (60 feet, 6 inches away from the pitcher). His job (usually) is to hit the cover off the ball that the pitcher throws to him. The hitter either reaches base and becomes a base-runner (which is a good thing), or makes an out (a bad thing) which is usually followed by the hitter walking back to the dugout with his head down amid a chorus of boos, hoots, cat calls, and so on.

Base runner – If the hitter does his job, he reaches base and becomes a base runner. His goal is to score a run (by advancing from 1st base to 2nd base, and on to 3rd base and finally to home plate).

Fielder – These are the guys in the field with gloves (besides the pitcher there are 8 of them scattered throughout the field). Their job is to "flash the leather" (ie. catch balls hit in their direction).

Starting Pitching Rotation

The heart of any pitching staff is its starting rotation, a collection of five pitchers who start every fifth game. They do this so they can rest their tired arms for 4 or 5 days in between starts.

Ace – Considered the best pitcher on the team, the anchor of the pitching staff. His blisters and hangnails make front-page news.

#2 Pitcher – Usually a cut below the ace (although on some blessed teams he can be just as good as the ace). His hangnails make back page news.

#3 Pitcher – A decent pitcher, likely an older pitcher who still can bring it, or a young rising star.

#4 Pitcher – Quality begins to suffer here. This might be an older, washed up pitcher who can grind out 5 innings for you. These guys are the most likely to be cheating – trying to get an edge.

#5 Pitcher – Many of these guys should be in the minor leagues, but aren't because (a) they are a young prospect who is getting his feet wet in the big leagues; (b) they have a big fat contract and the GM doesn't want to cut them; (c) they are left-handed (more on this later); (d) they have photos of the team's GM in a compromising position; (e) there's no one else better.

Relievers

Theoretically, if every starter pitched great and lasted the full 9 innings, you wouldn't need relievers. But starters get tired. They lose concentration. Sometimes they just have a bad day. For these reasons, every team has a cadre of pitchers who come into games when the starter falters and give the team a "pick-me-up." This group of pitchers are collectively referred to as "the bullpen," a reference to the place (a "pen" for humans) where relievers sit during the game.

Closer – The best pitcher in the bullpen. Sort of like the ace in the rotation. His job is to come into close games when his team is leading and get the last few outs to preserve the win. If he "saves" the game (there is a stat he can earn called a save), then everyone goes home happy. If he blows the lead and his team loses, he is a bum and is booed off the field. Only certain pitchers have the mentality to do this pressure-packed job well.

Set-up men – These guys usually come in an inning or two before the closer to provide quality pitching and to (in the best case) preserve a lead so that when the 9th inning rolls around, the closer still has a lead to protect.

Left-handed specialist – Every team has a left-handed specialist whose job is to face a dangerous left handed hitter at a crucial point late in the game. (Generally speaking, a left-handed hitter will find it more difficult to get a hit off a left-handed pitcher than a right-handed pitcher.) A decent "lefty" in the bullpen can make a million dollars a year facing only 50 batters in an entire season, or $20,000 per hitter faced.

Attention baseball fans: if you have a son who happens to be left-handed, get him out in the backyard throwing baseballs as early as possible. He is your "meal ticket" to retirement.

The rest of the bullpen – These pitchers are sometimes referred to as "mop-up men" or "inning-eaters". They come into games when their team has a big lead, or when the starter gets knocked out of the game early and the team needs someone to pitch 6 innings in a lost cause. Sometimes a guy from this group might get an emergency start if a starter is injured. No kid dreams of becoming one of these guys.

Position Players / Hitters

Catcher – Usually a big, burly, tree trunk type player. His job is to catch the pitcher, call the pitches, and throw out base runners when they try to steal.

First Baseman – Another big guy typically. His job is to catch the throws from his fellow infielders. Usually very social and will "chat up" opposing hitters who reach first base.

Second Baseman – Smaller and more agile than the first baseman, his primary job is to scoop up ground balls hit to him and throw them to the first baseman. Also needs to be able to turn the double play.

Shortstop – Usually the best defensive player on the team. Fast, agile, with a strong arm.

Third Baseman – Needs to be quick and have a strong arm (to throw all the way to first base). His area is called the "hot corner" because of the frequency of hard hit balls towards third base.

Left Fielder – The easiest of outfield positions. His job is to chew gum or tobacco, exchange jokes and/or profanity-laced insults with fans, and catch the occasional fly ball hit to him.

Center Fielder – Faster and more athletic than the left fielder, since he covers a much larger area.

Right fielder – Similar to the left fielder but generally a bit better defensively.

Bench Warmers – The rest of the team consists of hitters who wish they were position players but can't crack the starting lineup. These players pass the time in the dugout chewing tobacco, playing cards, insulting each other, and playing pranks. A classic baseball dugout prank is the "hot foot," where the instigator crawls under the bench, sticks some chewing gum onto another player's foot, and attaches a lit match to the gum, which results in a "hot foot".

Baseball 201

Baseball is a game of subtleties, and as you become more knowledgeable you'll begin to pick up nuances that your novice friends won't notice or appreciate. Here are some things to look for while you're watching a game.

Types of Pitches

"I use my single windup, my double windup, my triple windup, my hesitation windup, my no windup. I also use my step-n-pitch-it, my submariner, my sidearmer, and my bat dodger. Man's got to do what he's got to do." – Satchel Paige

To the baseball aficionado, the art of pitching – and the array of different pitches used to vanquish the opposing hitter – is a fascinating subject. It takes a well-trained eye to discern what type of pitch has been thrown (especially from a far away seat in the upper deck). However, as you become familiar with a pitcher's arsenal (pitchers usually have 3 or 4 pitches that they use regularly), you'll be able to tell during a game what pitch has been thrown (especially if you check the pitch speeds on the ballpark radar gun display).

Fastball – Also known as "the cheese" or "gas", the fastball is the bread-and-butter pitch for many pitchers. The average pitcher in the big leagues throws his fastball close to 90 MPH, while the most dominant pitchers can reach into the high 90's. Pitchers whose fastballs top out in the mid to high 80's will be in trouble unless they

have another pitch that hitters can't hit.

Curveball – Commonly referred to as "the hook". A curveball is gripped in such a way that the ball drops down and away as it crosses the strike zone.

Slider – Similar to the curve, but is thrown a lot faster and breaks more sharply.

Forkball / Split-fingered Fastball – This pitch became fashionable in the mid 1980s. To hitters, the forkball looks like a fastball but drops sharply just as the hitter attempts to swing at it.

Change-up – One of the keys to successful pitching is to change speeds so that the hitter's timing is disrupted. The change-up is thrown with an arm motion that looks a fastball, yet the ball leaves the pitchers hand at a speed 10-20 MPH slower than the fastball.

Knuckleball – A difficult pitch to throw, but if thrown correctly this pitch can be so devastating that even the catcher has trouble handling it. The pitch is thrown in such a way that there is very little rotation of the ball, which causes it to "dance" as it travels towards the plate. Since the knuckleball is thrown at a pretty slow speed (60-70 MPH), a poorly thrown knuckleball becomes an easy-to-hit, batting practice pitch, prompting fans to regard the pitcher as a knucklehead.

Screwball – Similar to the slider but the ball breaks in the opposite direction. Made famous by Dodger great Fernando Valenzuela. Sometimes referred to as the "screwgie".

Doctored pitches – Cheating has been a part of baseball since its inception. In fact, in the early part of the century doctored balls (spit-balls, for example) were legal.

Nowadays, pitchers looking to gain an edge will try to doctor the ball by scuffing the surface with a sharp object. These scuff marks will alter the ball's flight just enough to confuse the hitter.

Pitch Selection and Strategy

Another subtlety to watch for is the unspoken communication (and strategy) occurring throughout the game between the pitcher and catcher. Of course it all starts well before game-time, when the two meet and strategize how they'll pitch each hitter, based on mountains of data, video tape, and past experience with each hitter. Of course, this is all worthless if the pitcher can't execute the game plan. For example, the strategy might have been to work the opposing team's lead-off hitter with fastballs, but if the pitcher has lost confidence in his fastball, or is tiring, he's not going to want to stick to the game plan. Or, sometimes the strategy just plain stinks: the plan might have been to work a particular hitter with a steady diet of curveballs, but after being tattooed for a homerun and 2 doubles, the last thing that pitcher will want to do is throw another curveball to that hitter.

Pitchers and catchers have a unique way of communicating during the game. Before each pitch the catcher will signal – with his free hand - the type of pitch he thinks should be thrown. Sometimes catchers will even paint their nails a dark color so that the pitcher can see the signs. The pitcher (peering in to see these daintily-painted nails) will then either accept the pitch suggestion, or shake his head in disagreement (often described as "shaking of the catcher.") When this happens the catcher will usually just suggest another pitch, or run out to the mound and actually talk to the pitcher.

The signs from the catcher are not always so secret. The opposing team will often try to "steal" the signs signaled by the catcher. The most common example of this is a runner at second base, who will try to steal the signs from his vantage point behind the pitcher. This drives pitchers crazy. Another less common form of stealing can come from the actual hitter, who might take a quick peek down at the catcher's hand. This kind of behavior is considered very "un-cool," and often results in a fastball thrown at the hitter's noggin.

Signs

Ever wonder what the fat guy is doing near the third base bag, rubbing his stomach, grabbing the rim of his hat, and touching his ear? I'm not referring to the drunken fan sitting in the stands near third base. I'm talking about the third base coach, who is relaying signs from the dugout to the hitter and runners.

The first question many fans ask is "What's he telling the

hitter and runners to do?" Depending on the situation, the third base coach might be signaling for a bunt, a hit-and-run play, or a stolen base. The hitter and runners must be on the same page for these plays to be effective. Another common question is "Why do they need to do all those crazy things with their arms and hands to call a simple play?" The answer is that most of the gestures and signals from the third base coach are meaningless, but there are one or two gestures embedded among the sequence that actually mean something. This is done to make it difficult for the opposing team to de-code the signs and figure out the play.

Runner on First

"One time I snuck a ball on with me and when I went to winding up, I threw one of them balls to first and one to second. I was so smooth I picked off both runners and fanned the batter without that ump or the other team even knowing it." – Satchel Paige

The natural tension that occurs in the pitcher-hitter confrontation becomes more complex with a base runner at first. With a man on first, the pitcher's focus is now divided between the hitter and the base runner.

If you look closely, you'll see a "cat and mouse" game emerge between the base runner and the pitcher. The runner will attempt to get a good lead off first base (a general practice, and critical if he plans to steal second base). The pitcher will try to keep him close by throwing over to first in what is called a "pick off move." As the pitcher prepares to throw the pitch, you'll see him peek over to first to see how large a lead the runner has. The catcher may also throw quickly over to first base after a pitch is thrown, just to keep the runner honest.

Another subtlety is the way the pitcher throws his pitches with a runner on base. With the bases empty pitchers generally throw with a full wind-up. With runners on base, however, the pitcher now throws "from the stretch" in a shortened wind-up, which speeds up his delivery and gives the base runner less time to steal second base. The trade off, of course, is that pitchers generally sacrifice some speed when pitching from the stretch.

A good base stealer can really get into the pitcher's head and distract him as he tries to focus on the hitter. This "game within a game" is one of the many subtleties in baseball that often goes unnoticed, but can really add to the richness of the game. So when that base runner reaches first base, take a close look!

CHAPTER FOUR

LIFE BEYOND YANKEE STADIUM

(YES, IT DOES EXIST)

Following the Yankees

When you're not at Yankee Stadium you can still follow the Yankees on TV for those important 3-game series against arch-rivals. You can catch most of the Yankees game on WNYW channels. Check your local TV listings for the correct station.

Another option is to listen to the game on the radio. There's nothing quite like the experience of imagining the play on the field as the radio announcer paints a picture for you. Moreover, it's great background music that you can listen to while you're doing other stuff. It's tough to remain on the edge of your seat for three hours if you're not at the park. That's why TV or radio work so well while you're doing other things.

Finally, you can find Yankees information on the internet. Just surf your way to **www.yankees.com.**

Minor League Baseball - Class A
Staten Island Yankees

A great alternative to Yankee Stadium is a trip to the Yankees' single-A farm team, the Staten Island Yankees. While the Columbus Clippers represent a higher grade of baseball (AAA level), you'd have to travel all the way to Ohio to see the team. The SI Yanks, however, are local, so you can make the trip without too much driving.

Watching a game at Richmond County Bank Ballpark (RCBK Ballpark) is great because you're guaranteed good seats and a great waterfront view. It's cheap and you'll be away from all the hustle and bustle of the big leagues.

Getting to RCBK Ballpark is easy. From Manhattan, Brooklyn, Queens and Long Island, take the Verrazano Bridge to the Hylan Boulevard exit. Make a right onto Hylan Blvd, and follow Hylan to Bay Street. Make a left onto Bay Street and take Bay Street a little over 2 miles past the Staten Island Ferry terminal until you reach the Ballpark.

Tickets are cheap. General admission seats are only $8, and for you big spenders box seats are $10. To purchase tickets call (718) 720-9265.

Spring Training Baseball

For those of you craving Yankees baseball by March, you might want to make a trip to Tampa, Florida and take in some games at Legends Field. This beautiful spring training facility holds 10,000 fans, offers tickets at a somewhat reasonable $10, and even sports a mini-Monument Park. The Yankees have been known to sell out all their spring training games, so if you're planning a trip to Florida, try to buy your tickets in advance. Your best place to start is by visiting www.yankees.com, where you'll find ticket information.

Yogi Berra-isms

Any Yankee fan worth his salt is familiar with the often-quoted Yogi Berra, the great Yankee catcher-turned-philosopher. Here are some of Yogi's best.

On hitting:

- "He hits from both sides of the plate. He's amphibious."

- "So I'm ugly. I never saw anyone hit with his face."

- "I never blame myself when I'm not hitting. I just blame the bat and if it keeps up, I change bats. After all, if I know it isn't my fault that I'm not hitting, how can I get mad at myself?"

On the fans:

- "I don't know (if they were men or women fans running naked across the field). They had bags over their heads."

- "If people don't want to come out to the ballpark, how are you going to stop them?"

On parenting:

- "I'm not going to buy my kids an encyclopedia. Let them walk to school like I did."

On the fans:

- "All pitchers are liars or crybabies."

- "Baseball is ninety percent mental. The other half is physical."

CHAPTER FIVE

FANHOOD CHALLENGE

Multiple Choice Quiz

1. The "Old Yankee Stadium" featured a dark green screen which was used to:

   a. Shield the outfield fans from the sun or rain

   b. Honor St. Patrick's Day

   c. Give Yankee hitters an advantage over visiting hitters

   d. Prevent the blue outfield facade from clashing with the seats

   e. Help the grounds crew grow the grass to a dark green color

2. "The Monuments" of Ruth, Huggins, and Gehrig made it difficult for outfielders because:

   a. They were located in the outfield and could obstruct play

   b. Many outfielders were "spooked" by the historic plaques

   c. They cast a shadow over deep centerfield

   d. Visiting outfielders thought the monuments were actual teammates on the field

   e. They often toppled over and crushed helpless outfielders

3. Roger Maris hit his 61st homerun in:

   a. 1961

   b. 1927

   c. 1936

   d. little league

   e. 1967

4. The best way to order tickets on game day is to:

   a. Show up at Gate 6 and tell security that a Red Sox fan stole your tickets.

   b. Dress up in your Yankee uniform and go through the players entrance

   c. Look for scalpers

   d. Purchase them at the Advance Ticket Window

   e. Give up

5. "Death Valley" was named after:

   a. The visiting team's dugout

   b. Deep left/center field

   c. Craig Nettles' stinky locker

   d. Yankee Stadium bathrooms

   e. George Steinbrenner's Office

6. Yankee Stadiums smallest crowd of 413 fans occurred in:

    a. 1941 during World War II

    b. 1923 during Yankee Stadium's first year

    c. 1993 against the hapless Cleveland Indians

    d. 1966 against the White Sox

    e. 1952 after Joe DiMaggio retired

7. If you must buy scalped tickets, you should:

    a. Attach a sign to your chest reading "Need to buy illegal tickets"

    b. Stand around looking for the slick-looking people murmuring "tickets, tickets"

    c. Ask a police officer where you buy the tickets from scalpers

    d. Turn hat inside-out

    e. None of the above

8. The Yankees prohibit the following items from being brought into the Stadium:

    a. Can of Sprite

    b. Bottle of root beer

    c. A cooler with your lunch in it

    d. Any bag or backpack

    e. All of the above

9. The pitcher throws a 95 mph fastball close to the batter's face. This is called:

   a. A purpose pitch

   b. A scroogie

   c. A dinger

   d. An ohfer

   e. A spitball

10. Yankee Stadium was nicknamed "The House That Ruth Built" because:

    a. Ruth's cousin was it's construction foreman

    b. Ruth dictated its dimensions to team management

    c. Yankee Stadium was built by Ruth & Hamaker Construction

    d. It was built to showcase Ruth's talent

    e. The roof facade looked very similar to Ruth's childhood home

11. Casey Stengel's famous quote, "Ruth, Gehrig, Huggins, someone throw that darned ball in here, now!" occurred:

    a. When the three hall-of-famers were horsing around with a football in the locker room

    b. During an infield drill in spring training

    c. When a ball was hit into center field among the monuments

    d. After Stengel lost his cool during pre-game drills in the 1937 World Series

    e. During an amateur try-out for the three rookies

12. "Ruthville" and "Gehrigville" were named after:

a. The neighborhoods that Ruth and Gehrig lived in

b. The home dugout

c. Ruth's and Gehrig's lockers

d. Right and Left Field

e. The right field bleachers

13. During the 1974-1975 renovation of Yankee Stadium, the Yankees:

a. Played all their games on the road

b. Played their home games at nearby Shea Stadium

c. Cancelled the 1974 and 1975 seasons

d. Played their games in the Stadium, but no fans were allowed in

e. Reduced ticket prices to $1 for those fans willing to watch games amid the construction

ANSWERS

	7. b
13. b	6. d
12. e	5. b
11. c	4. d
10. d	3. a
9. a	2. a
8. e	1. c

SCORING

0–3 correct	Lost Devil Rays Fan
4–7 correct	"Standing-room-only" peon
8–10 correct	Bleacher bum
11–13 correct	Yankee Stadium Connoisseur

Yankee Stadium Puzzle

Find the 14 hidden words.

```
M  T  B  R  O  N  X  R  K  S  R  Q  L
O  A  L  W  G  Q  O  B  G  W  K  S  E
N  K  X  B  C  D  G  U  P  C  B  T  Z
U  A  Y  L  U  B  A  L  L  K  L  R  J
M  Y  B  E  T  S  J  L  S  J  E  I  L
E  C  R  A  E  X  S  P  J  N  J  K  E
N  K  L  C  T  F  E  E  T  B  N  E  R
T  J  S  H  W  W  N  N  B  R  A  D  S
S  N  D  E  A  T  H  V  A  L  L  E  Y
B  T  M  R  N  M  O  R  H  U  H  P  O
R  F  I  S  C  O  W  D  U  G  O  U  T
U  C  S  K  K  U  S  I  T  E  M  F  A
W  U  E  E  G  N  P  N  R  H  E  Z  T
G  R  K  G  Z  D  B  G  E  J  R  V  E
L  V  L  B  A  G  L  E  K  T  J  O  R
A  E  R  B  A  B  E  R  U  T  H  X  P
```

ANSWER

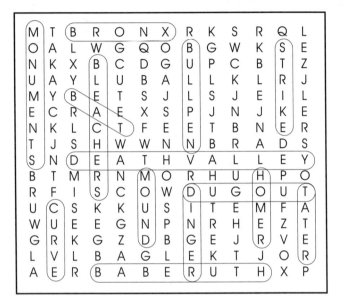

Yankee Stadium in Your Pocket Survey

Please take a moment to fill out this survey and send it to our address (shown at the bottom of survey) or email your answers and comments to ballparks2@aol.com. If we use your feedback, we'll give you official recognition in the next edition of this book.

Name (optional): _____

Address (optional): _____

_____

_____

Gender: ❏M ❏F

Age range: ❏ under 18 ❏ 18–25 ❏ 26–40 ❏ 40+

What best describes you?
❏ local Yankee fan
❏ out of towner visiting the New York area
❏ other _____

Why did you buy the guide? (Check all that apply)
❏ souvenir of Yankee Stadium
❏ useful info on planning a trip to the Stadium
❏ fun stuff to read about the Yankees
❏ I didn't buy it, it was given to me as a gift
❏ other _____

How have you been using the guide? (Check all that apply)
❏ read once for fun and put away
❏ use to plan trips to Yankee Stadium
❏ take it with me to the game
❏ other_____

Please share your personal tips and secrets to enjoying a game at Yankee Stadium below. If we use your tips we will recognize you in the next edition of this book.

_____
_____
_____
_____
_____
_____
_____
_____
_____
_____
_____

Please let us know if there's any way we can improve this guide. _____

_____
_____
_____
_____
_____
_____
_____
_____
_____

Thanks for your valuable input!

Mail survey to: Baseball Direct, P.O. Box 6463, Central Falls, RI 02863, or email us at ballpaks2@aol.com.